the journey's the thing
companion workbook

your guided journal for
well being and self-discovery

contains 52 weekly journaling prompts

dera nevin

QUENTIN IMPRINTS
NEW YORK CITY, NEW YORK

THE JOURNEY'S THE THING COMPANION WORKBOOK
Quentin Imprints, New York, NY

Editing, proofreading, cover design, and interior book design provided by Indigo: Editing, Design, and More:
Proofreader: Monte Lin
Cover and interior designer: Olivia M. Hammerman
www.indigoediting.com

ISBN: 979-8-9876460-5-2
Library of Congress Control Number: 2025920494

Contents

About This Workbook

Hi! My name is Dera. I am so excited that you're holding this workbook! You're taking an important step in a journey of self-discovery by developing a regular journaling practice. Whether this is your first-ever journal, your first journal containing prompts, or you are experienced with various forms of journaling, you are taking your place in a vibrant community of journalers!

Journaling is a fun pastime, but it also has many benefits when done as a practice. Regular journaling provides you with the space to **work through your thoughts and feelings** about the people and world around you, a practice which can **improve clarity and self-confidence**. The pages of a journal provide a **place for private self-reflection**, giving you a mirror into who you are and contributing to your **personal growth**. And in this always-on age, journaling—especially on paper—gives you a **personal space to pause and collect yourself** and your thoughts without judgment or haste.

This workbook contains 52 prompts and follows the journaling path and approach that I took as I wrote *The Journey's the Thing*. This workbook can be used for daily, weekly, or periodic practice. When I used the prompts contained in this workbook, I wrote on a weekly basis. Every Monday I'd choose a prompt and then write on that topic for 12 minutes a day, every day for a week. The next week I'd move onto a new prompt.

If you look, you can see that each prompt is divided into seven sections using a ∞. This is an aspirational place that you can get to in each writing session and is intended to mirror about 12- minutes of writing. You can choose to stop at that point or keep on going or even do less each day. It's up to you!

If I'm honest, there were some days when I was writing *The Journey's the Thing* that I skipped writing, but I always made it up by writing for two 12-minute intervals the next day, or some other time that week. If you've read that book, you'll see some essays are longer. On those weeks, there were days that I wrote longer than 12 minutes, or the writing just came quicker.

At the end of each week, or periodically, I'd go back and re-read what I wrote, and edit it a bit to tie everything together. I find re-reading helpful to put me back in touch with what I was thinking and feeling at the time. I often see things in a different light, and can find generosity with myself, and understanding and compassion. Sometimes things that had me upset or confused become more manageable when I look at them again with a bit of distance. In that way, journaling has helped me get clearer about the things I have written about, and that often helps me to feel better.

The process of journaling is intended to be flexible, and yours. If you're not feeling a prompt, skip elsewhere in the workbook to find one that works better for you. I've also suggested alternative prompts in some cases. You can also scratch out the prompt and add your own. Similarly, skip days if needed, and write more or less than suggested. There's no right way to do this, only the write way—the way that keeps you writing!

What I like about journaling is that it gives me personal space for self-expression. I can work through what I am thinking and feeling without judgment. I try to find a quiet time and space to write. Figure out what works for you: what writing tool you want to use, and to discover where and when you prefer to write. Just remember this doesn't need to be perfect and can be as messy as you want and need. Don't worry about grammar or spelling, or what anything looks like. This workbook is yours, to use as you want.

Sometimes, though, journaling might get hard. You might be busy or tired or sick. You might not feel like it. Some prompts may feel challenging, or you may get emotional. I used the prompts that are included in this workbook, and I found some of them hard to write about, but wrote anyway, including through my discompfort. All of this is normal and valuable. It may be helpful to journal about and through these situations. Get curious: How do you feel about being so busy? What's blocking you from writing? What do you find hard about writing, or about a prompt? Dig into the feelings that you feel and describe them. Messy, incomplete, and bad writing is still valuable and part of the process.

The practice of journaling can become a rewarding journey of self-discovery, fun to do, and rewarding uplifting to those that pursue it as a practice for its own sake. Journaling as a practice gifts you time, space, and clarity. In a quiet space of 12 minutes a day, you can show up for yourself, practice self-care and personal growth, and define who you are. It can help you make sense of yourself, those you care about and love, and the world you live in. Journaling can be especially helpful in navigating change, grief, and uncertainty. Going back through your journals from time to time might help you see patterns in what your life that you didn't see at the time. It can be a great way to get perspective.

I hope you enjoy and benefit from journaling, and this workbook. If you've found it helpful, consider encouraging someone else to give it a try. And join the vibrant community of people who are growing and thriving from the practice of journaling.

This workbook is not a substitute for counseling, coaching, therapy, or any other mental health service.

Guidance for Journaling

Here are some tips to help you get started in your journaling, and that can help you get unstuck if you ever find yourself at a loss for words.

12 Minutes a Day: Just Start, But Keep It Defined

Journaling can seem intimidating. You open a blank journal and see.... empty space. What do you write, and when do you stop?

I have found that setting a timer and writing for a defined period can help. I chose 12 minutes, because that's long enough that I could write a few sentences, but not so long that it interrupted my morning routine. The 12-minute block was suggested to me because that was the length of time that a tea I enjoyed drinking needed to steep: I started writing during those 12 minutes to pass the time. At the end of the 12 minutes, I had two rewards: some words completed on a page, and a delicious cup of tea.

Choosing a defined period to write in takes some of the thinking (and anxiety) away and may contribute to just helping you get started. Just pick an interval of time that's meaningful enough to get some words down. During that period, just write. When the timer goes off, just stop. Or don't. Up to you.

As you get more experienced, you can decide to extend the interval. Or not. Up to you.

Tactical Journaling: Be Intentional

In addition to defining an interval of time in which to write, I also define a subject to write about by using a prompt. I call this Tactical Journaling. Because I find this technique helpful, this workbook includes weekly prompts to help you get writing. Starting from a prompt helps to define the writing activity, and encourages action.

Instead of approaching an empty page, the prompt is the starting line and reference point for my thoughts. It is the thing I can write about, and what I can return to, during the defined writing period if I get stuck or off-topic. The prompt helped me to focus on a topic that I wanted to explore, or was suggested to me (by friends, by current events, by opening a piece of writing and randomly choosing a word). Using a word or idea to write about can be a gentle way to explore thoughts and feelings about the world without just having to emote on the page.

I keep the prompts simple, and use a word or a short phrase, so I can take it in any direction I choose to go.

Writing in The Age Of AI:
You Must Use Your Mind To Know It

I get asked the question: Why write at all now that we have Generative AI (and Large Language Models) that can generate text for us when we give this technology a prompt. Why not just take the prompts in this workbook and input those into the Generative AI, which can do the writing work for us?

I respond: You must use your mind to know it. And writing is a technique you can use to know your mind. Writing requires you to think through and record your own ideas. If the purpose of prompting is just to generate any text at all, then use a Generative AI tool. That technology is designed to generate text, and it will do so, using its billions of parameters of training data to create plausible-seeming ideas. But are the words that result from the Generative AI prompt what you think, or what you believe, or how you really feel?

Especially if you don't know whether what the Generative AI presents is totally aligned with your own thinking and feelings, it's important for you to go through your own generation and creation process to discover this for yourself, and you can do this by writing. Use your own mind and vocabulary to come up with your own answers. Journaling can help you do this.

Journaling is not an outcome. The act of journaling *is* the valuable process, as is belonging to a community of practice, and of sharing your experience of the process with others going through it and comparing notes. What humans can do that machines can't is relate to themselves and each other. Journaling is an activity that defines us as human, and helps to improve us as humans.

Journaling is a response to the Age of AI. Understand and define yourself by and through writing. Know (and control) your own mind.

When Writing Gets Hard: Write Anyway

The incredible thing about journaling as a daily or periodic practice is that its momentum can help you when things get hard. Just write anyway.

Write about how hard it is to write. Write about how you don't want to write. Write about how you feel about not writing. Write about why writing is a waste of time. Write about anyone telling you you're not doing it right, and parrot back any criticism you are getting, including from yourself or your inner voices, and write down your reactions to that.

If external situations are making it hard for you to write, such as family obligations, illness, job loss, anxiety, errands, or other obligations, then take even just a minute, and write about that. What's going on, and why? How is all this affecting you and those around you? Describe it.

If you're had to miss a bit of writing, when you come back to it, write about that. What happened? What was it like to miss writing? What's it like to be back writing again?

When writing gets hard, write anyway. There's always something to write about.

Piecing It Together: You Can Fix It Later

The best writing is written, and then re-written (probably multiple times). Editing writing is a different process than writing.

That's good news. It means that when you are writing, you can just write. You don't need to worry about spelling, or grammar, or if it makes sense, or what it looks like. It doesn't have to be perfect, it just needs to be expressive, whatever that looks like. You can cross things out, write outside the lines and in the margins, use the page however you want.

And, if you decide, later, you can go back to it and fix it. You can type it into a computer or revise it on another page. You can fix spelling and grammar errors or rephrase things. You can change your mind about ideas you expressed or put new words against the same ideas because you understand things differently.

It's OK. Returning to writing later, stitching it together, editing it, revising it is all part of the process. It doesn't have to happen all at once.

You don't even have to fix it later. Your first draft can be your only draft. It's your journal, and it's up to you.

Reflecting Back:
Review Your Work to Review Your Progress

Whether or not you return to your work to review it for revision, you can reread what you wrote to better understand yourself and what you were thinking and going through. Looking back on journals can offer you a mirror into your thoughts, situations, and feelings, and give you perspective on your own journey and process of personal growth.

Even if you don't go back and reread the entries in this workbook, taking a periodic inventory of where you are at, and contemplating what's next for you, will offer you the space for self-reflection. The journal reflects the process, and the history behind how and who you are becoming.

Reviewing your journal can provide insight into your patterns of behavior and feelings, how you spend your time, what you want and need more of, and what you think about your life and the world you live in. Just as looking in a mirror gives you important information about how you look and how you might look to others, looking back in your journal will reflect parts of your inner life to you.

You can review parts or all of your journal now or years from now. Up to you.

Your journal is both the map and the record of your journey. Enjoy it! Most importantly: *the journey's the thing.*

52 Journaling Prompts

On Starting

_____

_____

_____

_____

_____

_____

_____

_____

_____

_____

∞

_____

_____

_____

_____

_____

_____

_____

_____

_____

_____

_____

∞

_____

_____

_____

_____

_____

_____

_____

_____

_____

_____

_____

∞

_____

_____

_____

_____

That I am starting this journey at all is the victory.

On Staying

8

∞

∞

And now that it's declared, it's decided—because there's a power in such moments.

On Comparing

_____

_____

_____

_____ ∞

_____

_____

_____

_____

_____

_____

_____

_____

_____

_____

_____

_____ ∞

_____

_____

_____

Where I am exactly now is the best manifestation of who and how I am, because that is, in fact, who and how I am.

On Deciding

∞

∞

∞

There is freedom and grace in taking a decision and trying.

On Running
Alternative prompt: On Passion

8

∞

∞

There is something about shared activity... that deepens vulnerability and opens hearts.

On Belonging

∞

∞

∞

In belonging, we square our edges into the whole, and we will fit, even imperfectly.

On Faith

∞

∞

Faith is inherently generative and renewable.

Reflection

It's a helpful reminder that acting with integrity is now and always the sole project and purpose of life. It's how you acquire knowledge of what's important to you and what you consent to doing with your time, talents, and intentions, and then to act with courage to bring those things to being, and to trust in them.

On Exhaustion

∞

On Starting Over

∞

∞

∞

It's been the best and most catastrophic thing I have done. Exhilarating, liberating, frustrating, isolating, exhausting.

On What I Haven't Done

∞

∞

∞

How you spend your time every day is what makes you who you are.

On Adjustment

∞

∞

∞

Although the one constant in life is change, we often choose against it.

On Masks

8

∞

∞

What we portray is never the whole of who we are, which encompasses the gap between what we show and what others see.

Reflection

Do you know what it's like to feel really seen?

On Courage

∞

∞

Courage is an act of heart-strength.

On Duty

∞

On Perseverance

∞

∞

∞

The reason for failure in most cases is lack of perseverance.

On Fragility

∞

On Memories

∞

∞

∞

The only thing that is ever slipping away is time. Objects and people just come and go, sometimes passing through our lives where journeys intersect in space and time.

On Marriage
Alternative prompt: On Relationships

∞

∞

∞

On Gratitude

∞

∞

∞

I am humbled by how much we take our ordinary things for granted.

On Teaching

∞

On Impermanence

∞

∞

∞

For most of us, a legacy is not a thing that we do but a series of habits we practice.

On Disgust

∞

∞

Disgust serves a critical function to keep us safe from toxins, but it can play havoc when we are not really at risk.

On Risk

∞

∞

Risk, then, is an invitation not to adventure, but to knowledge.

Reflection

We wager big when we understand what's at stake—what we have to win and what we have to lose—but also when we understand how to calibrate our energies and resources, when we are able to take aim, and when we recognize how and where our adventure lands. We cannot live without risk and the attention it demands—it is the thing that makes life alive!

On Togetherness

∞

On Grace

∞

∞

∞

Grace is available if we have courage to receive it.

On Joy

On Boundaries

∞

∞

∞

Boundaries create distinctions, which can bring into focus that which we need to see.

On Writer's Block
Alternative prompt: On Being Stuck

∞

On Change

∞

∞

∞

Little changes, consistently applied, can add up.

On Birds, Trees, Flowers, and Owls
Alternative prompt: On My Neighborhood

∞

_____

_____

_____

_____ ∞

_____

_____

_____

_____

_____

_____

_____

_____

_____ ∞

_____

_____

_____

_____

To live life tree by tree, bird by bird, flower by flower. And one magnificent owl at a time.

On Overwhelm

On Perspective

∞

∞

∞

Perspective is the maturation of our being in the world.

On Procrastination

∞

∞

∞

When we put something off that is a priority for us, we add noise to our lives.

On Burnout

∞

Reflection

But I am also reminded that intentional action is paramount. There is no substitute for creating space in life to do the things that are meaningful, and space takes boundaries.

On Destruction

∞

∞

∞

On Foundations

∞

∞

∞

Anything worthwhile is built on a foundation, even if we don't see it, and establishing a foundation takes time, discipline, and focus. It's about showing up not once, but over and over again.

∞

∞

On Cowardice

∞

∞

∞

∞

On Revolutions

∞

∞

∞

Change is constant. Change is hard. And change is our purpose in life. We think we can change by reaction and inattention. But the transformation happens with attention, action, and purpose.

∞

∞

On Believing

∞

∞

∞

What we do matters.

∞

∞

On Volunteering

∞

∞

By the act of volunteering, we can change the world and how we show up in it and change ourselves for those we choose to have in our lives.

On Poetry
Alternative prompt: On Art

∞

On Mourning

∞

∞

∞

All grief marks an emotional injury, and grief can cut deep and leave permanent, though not always visible, scars.

∞

∞

On Stillness

8

∞

∞

In stillness, we stop and let the world in.

∞

∞

On Presence

∞

On Abundance

∞

On Time

∞

∞

What distinguishes a life is time: how time is understood, perceived, mediated, and used.

∞

∞

On Solitude

∞

∞

∞

On Confidence

∞

∞

∞

∞

∞

On Growth

∞

On Undoing
Alternative prompt: On Unlearning

∞

∞

∞

We live into the spaces we create from our imaginations through consistent diligence.

On Journaling

_____

_____

_____

_____

_____

_____

_____

_____

_____

_____

_____

_____

_____

_____

_____

_____

_____

_____

_____

_____

On What's Next

∞

∞

∞

What's Next

Congratulations! Whether you have completed all or some of the prompts in this workbook or decided that you are looking for more information to deepen your journaling practice, here are some suggestions for steps you can take next.

Deepening Your Practice:

- Set up a sustainable long-term routine (daily 12-minute sessions, weekly reflection rituals, etc.).

- Experiment with journaling using different formats: digital apps, voice recordings, or artistic or mixed-media (art and text) journaling.

- Set quarterly reflection sessions to review your journal entries for patterns and growth.

- Start another year with a new set of prompts or get another copy of this workbook and re-use the prompts to see what's changed for you and how you've grown!

- Create your own prompts based on what resonated most during the first 52 weeks.

- Transition to self-directed journaling without prompts, and trust the foundation you've built.

Sharing and Community Building:

- Share your experience or meaningful insights (while keeping personal details private) on social media using a hashtag like #My52WeekJourney.

- Write a review sharing how this workbook impacted your life. Your story could inspire others to start their own journey!

- Gift copies of this workbook (or bundle) to friends or family members who might benefit from developing a journaling practice.

- Start a journaling circle with friends or family to discuss insights and maintain accountability.

- Consider joining me and my community of journalers by connecting online and through social media.

Continuing your Education:

- There are other techniques for journaling, and you can explore these and whether they work for you.

- Read books by renowned journaling experts, mentors, and teachers.

- Take workshops or courses on advanced journaling techniques.

- Consider how journaling has prepared you for other reflective practices like meditation, or contributed to your personal or spiritual growth, or well-being. Consider writing about this in a journal entry!

My hope is that this workbook has inspired you to start journaling or deepen your practice.

Keep with it, keep connected, and keep journaling!

Acknowledgments

I am indebted to the community that reacted to *The Journey's the Thing* and asked that I turn the prompts into this workbook.

The idea was first Stacey's, and it's on me that it took me some time to understand her perspective. I am also grateful to early draft workbook readers Stacey, Melissa, Corrie, Brian, Valerie, A., and Sharon G. You improved this workbook from your suggestions and support. I am grateful for my writing crew Valerie, Janice, and Ari, my work and professional cheerleaders Kiley, Tracy, Peter, and Doug, and my all-purpose crew of Corrie, Mark, Daniel, Alex, Cathy, Allison, Penelope, Chris, Robert, and Brian. Michael has remained a friend and supporter of Quentin Imprints, this workbook's publisher, even as we've gone running around in countless circles.

And big love to mum and dad, my first and forever cheerleaders.

About the Author

Photograph by Giancarlo Osaben

Dera Nevin began keeping a diary at the age of nine. Born into an unconventional family, she learned to process her emotions and make sense of the world around her by writing.

As an adult, she became a lawyer, and learned how to handle high-stakes situations and help her clients navigate life's challenges as a trusted advisor. After several busy and difficult years in a row, during which she was confronted by multiple work, health, and family challenges, Dera started journaling off and on again to try and find her own clarity and peace of mind.

Then during the pandemic year of 2020, she unlocked a journaling technique, Tactical Journaling, in which she recommitted to a consistent daily journal practice of at least twelve minutes a day. The practice left her calmer, more focused, and energized, and she found renewed purpose in her writing. As she started to share her journal entries once a week on social media, she realized that her journal prompting techniques were inspiring to those around her. Dera is now the founder of Quentin Imprints LLC, a company dedicated to personal discovery and expression.

You can connect with Dera on social media and at www.deranevin.com.

www.ingramcontent.com/pod-product-compliance
Lightning Source LLC
Chambersburg PA
CBHW082247120626
46555CB00009B/2991